Pennie Stoyles and Christine Mulvany

The A–Z of
Scientific
Discoveries

Volume 4 M–O

Smart Apple Media

Smart Apple Media
P.O. Box 3263
Mankato, MN, 56002

First published in 2009 by
MACMILLAN EDUCATION AUSTRALIA PTY LTD
15–19 Claremont Street, South Yarra, Australia 3141

Visit our web site at www.macmillan.com.au or go directly to www.macmillanlibrary.com.au

Associated companies and representatives throughout the world.

Copyright © Pennie Stoyles and Christine Mulvany 2009

Library of Congress Cataloging-in-Publication Data

Stoyles, Pennie.
　　The A to Z of scientific discoveries / Pennie Stoyles and Christine Mulvany.
　　　　p. cm.
　　Includes index.
　　ISBN 978-1-59920-445-1 (hardcover)
　　ISBN 978-1-59920-446-8 (hardcover)
　　ISBN 978-1-59920-447-5 (hardcover)
　　ISBN 978-1-59920-448-2 (hardcover)
　　ISBN 978-1-59920-449-9 (hardcover)
　　ISBN 978-1-59920-450-5 (hardcover)
　　1. Discoveries in science--Encyclopedias, Juvenile. I. Mulvany, Christine. II. Title.
　　Q180.55.D57S76 2010
　　503--dc22

　　　　　　　　　　　　2009003443

Edited by Kath Kovac
Text and cover design by Ivan Finnegan, iF Design
Page layout by Ivan Finnegan, iF Design
Photo research by Legend Images
Illustrations by Alan Laver, Shelly Communications
Solar system illustrations (pp 6, 8, 20) by Melissa Webb

Printed in the United States

Acknowledgments
The author and the publisher are grateful to the following for permission to reproduce copyright
material:

Front cover photograph: Astronaut on the moon courtesy of Digital Vision

Photos courtesy of: AAP/EPA/Wu Hong, **26**; Digital Vision, **14**, **15** (right); © Ceras/Dreamstime.
com, **22**; © Gezafarkas/Dreamstime.com, **23** (left); Mike Brinson/Getty Images, **17** (right);
Jose Luis Pelaez/Getty Images, **30**; © Calvin J. Hamilton, **7** (bottom); © Marie-france Bélanger/
iStockphoto, **27** (center); © Jeremy Edwards/iStockphoto, **18** (top); Library of Congress,
13; NASA/Johns Hopkins University Applied Physics Laboratory/Carnegie Institution of
Washington, **9**; NASA/JPL, **21** (top); NASA/JPL-Caltech/University of Arizona, **7** (top);
Photolibrary/Science Photo Library, **18** (bottom); Photolibrary/Pekka Parviainen/Science Photo
Library, **10**; Photolibrary/Royal Astronomical Society/Science Photo Library, **21** (bottom);
Photos.com, **16** (bottom); © AGPhotographer/Shutterstock, **23** (right); © Perry Correll/
Shutterstock, **28**; © Dhoxax/Shutterstock, **29** (right); © Pichugin Dmitry/Shutterstock, **11**; ©
Jostein Hauge/Shutterstock, **27** (right); © Karin Lau/Shutterstock, **19**; © Ronen/Shutterstock,
17 (left); © SandiMako/Shutterstock, **29** (left); © Tatonka/Shutterstock, **24**; © TheSupe87/
Shutterstock, **27** (left); U.S. Air Force photo by Senior Airman Joshua Strang, **5** (bottom)

Scientific Discoveries

Welcome to the Exciting World of Scientific Discoveries.

The A–Z of Scientific Discoveries is about the discovery and explanation of natural things. A scientific discovery can mean:

- finding or identifying something that exists in nature
- developing a theory that helps describe and explain a natural thing or event

A scientific discovery is sometimes the work of one person. Sometimes it is a series of discoveries made by many people building upon each other's ideas.

Volume 4 M–O   Scientific Discoveries

They Said It!

"No great discovery was ever made without a bold guess."

Isaac Newton, English scientist who discovered the laws of motion

Magnetic Poles

The North and South Magnetic Poles are areas that have the most intense magnetic fields on Earth's surface.

Awareness of the Magnetic Poles

People may have known about the magnetic poles for thousands of years. A 3000-year-old **hematite** artifact, thought to be a magnetic direction finder, was created by a civilization that lived in the area now known as Mexico. Scientists developed an interest in Earth's magnetic field in the 1800s. In 1849, French physicist Achilles Delasses discovered that rocks were magnetized parallel with Earth's magnetic field.

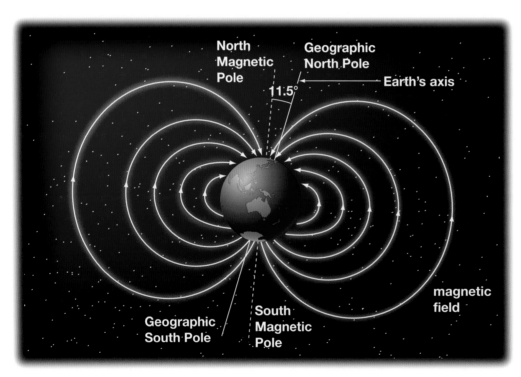

The magnetic poles move around over time and are currently about 11 degrees from Earth's axis.

Origin of the Magnetic Poles

Scientists have discovered that Earth's magnetic field is created within the liquid outer core that spins around the solid inner core, but they do not yet understand how.

Did You Know?

Animals that migrate long distances, such as thrush nightingales, are thought to navigate using Earth's magnetic field.

The beautiful auroras visible at the poles are caused when Earth's magnetic field traps particles from the solar wind – a stream of high-speed charged particles ejected from the sun.

Discovery that the Magnetic Poles Shift

In the past, the magnetic poles have reversed from north to south. In 1906, French physicist Bernard Brunhes found rocks that were magnetized in the opposite direction. However, suggestions of pole reversals were not taken seriously until the 1950s and 1960s, when scientists discovered **basalt** rock ridges on the sea floor that kept the magnetic direction of the time they formed. The poles have reversed 171 times at irregular intervals over the past 76 million years, but the reasons why the reversals occur have not yet been fully explained.

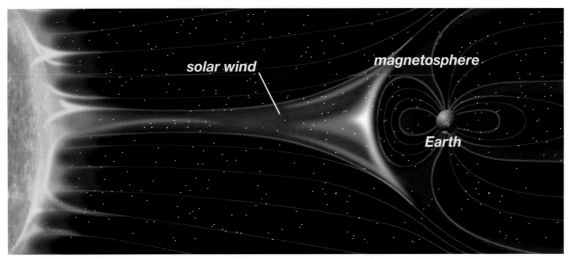

solar wind

magnetosphere

Earth

The magnetosphere, which is the part of Earth's magnetic field that extends into space, shields the planet from harmful solar winds from the sun.

Magnetic Poles in Everyday Life

A compass contains a magnetized pointer that points to the North Magnetic Pole. Compasses have been used in navigation for many years, but their use is now decreasing with the rise in Global Positioning System (GPS) technology.

GLOSSARY WORDS

hematite   a mineral that contains large amounts of iron
basalt   a hard, dark rock made from solidified lava

Mars

Mars is a small, rocky, reddish planet. It is the fourth planet from the sun.

How Mars and its Features Were Discovered

Mars is easily seen without a telescope, and so its discovery is not credited to one person. Galileo Galilei first viewed Mars through a telescope in 1609. In 1877, Italian astronomer Giovanni Virginio Schiaparelli observed straight channels on the planet's surface. This fueled the first suggestions of life on Mars. The most accurate information has been collected by spacecraft that have flown by, orbited, and landed on the planet's surface.

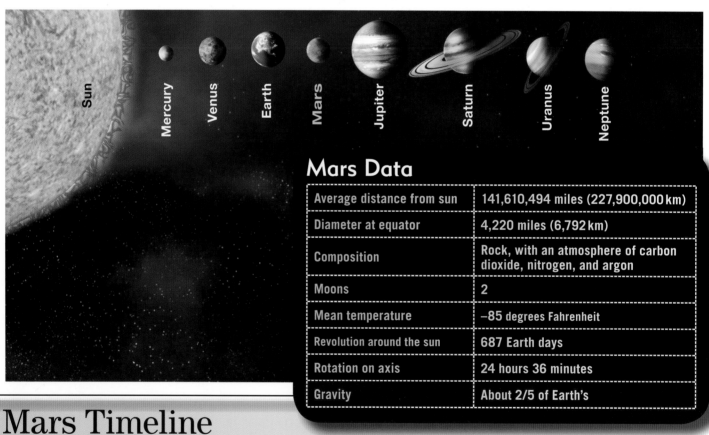

Sun · Mercury · Venus · Earth · Mars · Jupiter · Saturn · Uranus · Neptune

Mars Data

Average distance from sun	141,610,494 miles (227,900,000 km)
Diameter at equator	4,220 miles (6,792 km)
Composition	Rock, with an atmosphere of carbon dioxide, nitrogen, and argon
Moons	2
Mean temperature	−85 degrees Fahrenheit
Revolution around the sun	687 Earth days
Rotation on axis	24 hours 36 minutes
Gravity	About 2/5 of Earth's

Mars Timeline

1877	1965	1976	2004
American astronomer Asaph Hall discovered Phobos and Deimos, the two moons of Mars	The spacecraft *Mariner 4* took the first close-up pictures of Mars' surface	Spacecrafts *Viking 1* and *Viking 2* landed on Mars	Mars Expedition Rovers, *Spirit* and *Opportunity*, discovered the planet once had liquid water

Mars Missions

Since *Mariner 4*'s flyby of Mars in 1965, many spacecraft missions have added to our knowledge of the planet. In 1971, *Mariner 9* photographed the entire planet and took the first close-up pictures of the Martian moons, Phobos and Deimos. In 1997, *Mars Global Surveyor* collected data used to make a three-dimensional map of Mars as well as weather maps.

Viking 1 and **Viking 2** were the first spacecraft to land on the surface of Mars.

Three spacecraft – *Mars Odyssey*, *Mars Express*, and *Mars Reconnaissance Orbiter* – are currently orbiting Mars. The surface is also home to two Mars Exploration Rovers, *Spirit* and *Opportunity*, and the robotic lander *Phoenix*. In 2005, *Mars Express* took images of a possible frozen sea that may have been liquid five million years ago. The *Phoenix*, which landed in 2008, investigated the history of water on the planet. Astronomers predict that one day, people will be able to visit Mars.

The Martian moon Phobos was first photographed by the *Mariner 9* satellite.

Did You Know?

Mars is named after the Roman god of war. Its two moons are named after the horses that pulled his chariot: Phobos and Deimos.

Mercury

Mercury is a small, rocky planet that is closest to the sun.

How Mercury and its Features Were Discovered

Mercury was observed by people from ancient cultures. Its discovery is not credited to just one person. Telescopes have allowed closer examination, although Mercury's closeness to the sun makes it hard to see.

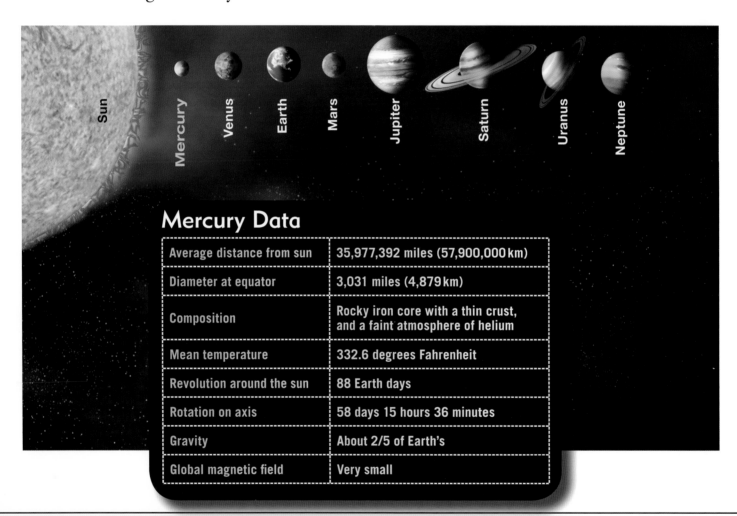

Sun Mercury Venus Earth Mars Jupiter Saturn Uranus Neptune

Mercury Data

Average distance from sun	35,977,392 miles (57,900,000 km)
Diameter at equator	3,031 miles (4,879 km)
Composition	Rocky iron core with a thin crust, and a faint atmosphere of helium
Mean temperature	332.6 degrees Fahrenheit
Revolution around the sun	88 Earth days
Rotation on axis	58 days 15 hours 36 minutes
Gravity	About 2/5 of Earth's
Global magnetic field	Very small

Mercury Timeline

1965	1974–75	2008	2011
Scientists discovered that the same side of Mercury does not always face the sun	*Mariner 10* photographed the planet's surface features	*MESSENGER's* closest fly-by produced close-up pictures of the unseen side of Mercury	*MESSENGER* will orbit Mercury

Mercury's Orbit

In the 1800s, scientists discovered that Mercury's orbit was very **elliptical**. The planet comes to within 29 million miles (46 million km) of the sun at its nearest approach, but at its furthest point, it is 44 million miles (70 million km) from the sun. People thought that another planet existed closer to the sun that affected Mercury's orbit. They nicknamed the missing planet Vulcan, but it was never found. Eventually, scientists used mathematics to explain Mercury's unusual orbit.

The *MESSENGER* (MErcury Surface, Space ENvironment, GEochemistry, and Ranging) spacecraft took this image of Mercury in 2008.

Did You Know?
Because Mercury moves quickly around the sun, it was named after the winged Roman god of travel.

GLOSSARY WORD

elliptical   oval-shaped

Meteorites

Meteorites are solid objects from space that pass through Earth's atmosphere and land on the surface.

Ancient Meteorite Discoveries

Since ancient times, meteorites have been collected as special stones by a range of cultures. Meteorites that were seen falling were thought to be from the gods and were often sacred objects. Many meteorites contain a lot of iron, so they were valuable stones for making spear tips and cutting tools.

Modern Discoveries

In the 1930s, American scientist Harvey Nininger started a systematic collection of meteorites for scientific study. Many countries now run projects to look for meteorites, because they hold valuable clues to the formation of the solar system. Most meteorites are thought to have come from the asteroid belt.

Meteors are space objects that burn up as they pass through the atmosphere and do not reach a planet's surface. Meteor showers can be seen when Earth passes through the orbit of a comet's tail.

Discovering the Largest-Known Meteorite

The largest-known meteorite was discovered accidentally in a field being ploughed on the Hoba farm, in Namibia, Africa. The Hoba meteorite weighs about 145,200 pounds (66,000 kg) and is about 9.8 feet (3 m) across.

The Hoba meteorite, which is mainly made of iron, hit Earth about 80,000 years ago.

Martian Meteorites

In 1984, members of the American Antarctic Search for Meteorites Program discovered a meteorite from Mars that reached Earth 13,000 years ago. The meteorite contains structures that could be fossilized **nanobacteria**, but this claim is not yet proven.

Did You Know?
Meteorites are named after the place where they are found.

GLOSSARY WORD

nanobacteria   bacteria measuring 200 billionths of a meter across

Molecules

Molecules are made up of two or more **atoms** joined by a chemical bond.

How Molecules Were Discovered

The discovery of molecules happened at the same time as the discovery of atoms. In 1625, French scientist René Descartes believed that atoms had tiny hooks and loops that held them together to make molecules. Other scientists thought that molecules were held together with a sort of glue. By 1803, English scientist John Dalton had discovered how many atoms made up some simple molecules.

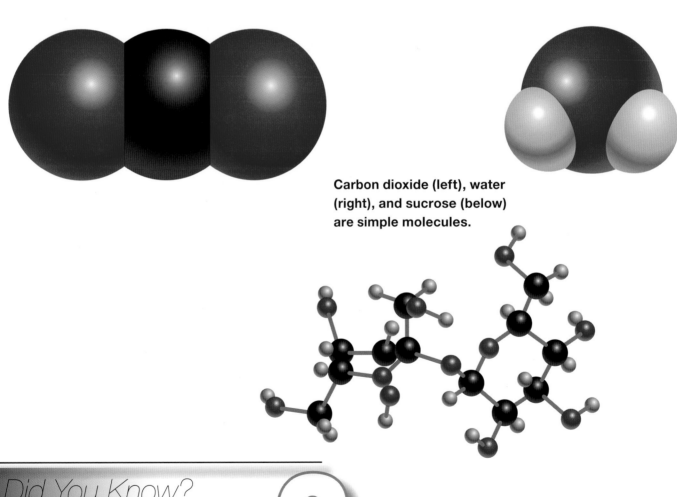

Carbon dioxide (left), water (right), and sucrose (below) are simple molecules.

Molecule Shapes

In 1857, German scientist Freidrich Kekulé discovered that each atom will only join to a certain number of other atoms. Oxygen can make two chemical bonds, carbon can make four, and hydrogen can make only one. In 1893, another German scientist, Alfred Werner, showed that the number of bonds determines a molecule's shape. In the 1920s and 1930s, American scientist Linus Pauling discovered that the chemical bonds holding atoms together were formed by the interaction of the atom's **electrons**.

Naming Molecules

A molecule's name and chemical formula reveal the number and type of atoms it contains. For example, a hydrogen sulfide (rotten eggs gas) molecule contains two hydrogen atoms and one sulphur atom. Its chemical formula is H_2S.

Linus Pauling (1901–1994) discovered how chemical bonds hold atoms together to form molecules, and worked out the structure of some complicated molecules found in the human body.

Moon

The Moon is a natural body that orbits Earth. Although it is the brightest object in the night sky, it does not produce any light of its own. It is lit by the sun.

Moon Discoveries of the Past

When the Moon's surface is viewed without a telescope, light and dark areas can be seen. The lava-filled craters, known as maria, are darker than the lighter areas of rugged highlands, called terrae. Early Greek astronomers falsely believed the dark areas were seas. The invention of the telescope allowed Galileo Galilei to first describe the Moon's surface in 1609. In 1645, Dutch astronomer Michael Florent van Langren produced the first map of the Moon's near side. American scientist John William Draper took the first photographs of the Moon in 1840.

Moon Data

Average distance from sun	238,606 miles (384,000 km)
Diameter at equator	2,159 miles (3,475 km)
Composition	Volcanic rock similar to Earth
Mean temperature	−4 degrees Fahrenheit
Revolution around the sun	27.3 Earth days
Rotation on axis	27 days 7 hours 42 minutes
Gravity	About 1/6 of Earth's

Moon Mission Timeline

1959	1966	1968	1969
Luna 2 spacecraft crashed onto the Moon's surface	*Luna 9* spacecraft had a soft landing on the Moon	*Apollo 8* spacecraft orbited the Moon with a human crew	*Apollo 11* spacecraft landed the first humans on the Moon

Lava-filled craters, or maria, are shown as darker areas in this satellite image of the Moon.

Moon Discoveries

In 1959, *Luna 1,* the first spacecraft to fly by the Moon, discovered that the Moon did not have a magnetic field. In the same year, *Lunar Orbiter 3* observed the **far side** of the Moon for the first time. As the Moon rotates at nearly the same speed at which it orbits Earth, only one side of the Moon is visible from Earth.

Between 1969 and 1972, 12 people walked on the moon's surface. The moon rocks they collected showed that the Moon and Earth were made from similar materials. NASA's Constellation project aims to return people to the Moon's surface by 2020.

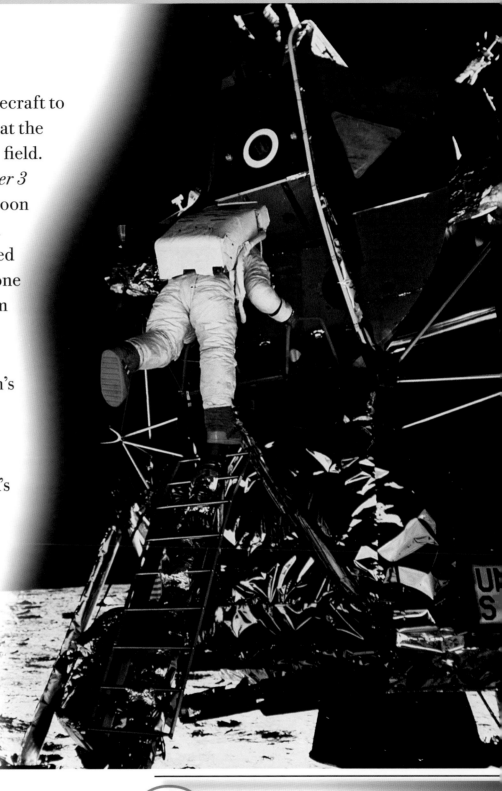

On July 20, 1969, Neil Armstrong took the first step on the Moon's surface.

Did You Know?

The Moon affects the size of the ocean tides on Earth.

GLOSSARY WORD

far side side of the Moon not visible from Earth

Motion

Motion is a change in position over time. The rules of motion explain why objects are located at a particular place at a particular time.

How the Theories of Motion Were Discovered

Like many scientific discoveries, the theories of motion were developed by different scientists building on previous ideas. In 1687, Sir Isaac Newton published his principles of gravity and the three laws of motion. His laws built upon ideas about objects at rest and the speed of falling objects proposed by Galileo Galilei in the 1500s. The laws also referred to Johannes Kepler's Laws of Planetary Motion, which were published around 1605.

Newton's First Law of Motion

Newton's first law is known as the law of inertia (say in-ERSH-a). It states that an object will remain at rest or moving steadily until another force acts upon it.

If a moving car stopped suddenly and you were not wearing a seatbelt, the law of inertia means you would move forward, hitting or even going through the windshield.

Sir Isaac Newton (1642–1727)

Sir Isaac Newton was a great English scientist and mathematician. He also developed the theory of gravity, furthered our understanding of optics, and helped to develop the branch of mathematics known as calculus.

Newton's Second Law of Motion

Newton's second law states that the change in the speed and/or direction of an object is related to the size of the force acting on it and the mass of the object. The larger the force acting on an object, the greater the change in speed and/or direction; and, the greater the mass of the object, the smaller the change in its speed and/or direction.

If two racing cars have the same engines, but different masses, the car with the smaller mass will increase its speed at a faster rate.

Newton's Third Law of Motion

The third law states that every action has an equal and opposite reaction. For example, if you release an air-filled balloon, the air is pushed out of the open nozzle. The air pushes back with an equal and opposite reaction, forcing the balloon to move in the opposite direction.

Newton's third law of motion explains that as the skateboarder pushes on the ground in one direction, the board and the skater are pushed by the ground in the opposite direction.

Neon is a colorless, odorless gas that is lighter than air. It is the fifth most common element in the universe, but is very rare on Earth.

How Neon Was Discovered

In the 1890s, scientists knew that air contained small amounts of gases other than nitrogen and oxygen. In 1898, Scottish chemist Sir William Ramsay and English chemist Morris Travers cooled an air sample until it became a liquid. They heated the liquid and captured three gases from it: neon, krypton, and xenon (say ZEN-on). When they passed an electric current through the neon gas, they saw a blaze of red light.

Las Vegas is famous for its neon lights.

Morris Travers (1872–1961)

Morris Travers became a professor of chemistry in 1903. He went to India in 1906 as head of the Indian Institute of Scientists, but returned to Britain when World War I began. He continued to study gases, and became interested in cryogenics – the study of very cold things.

More About Neon

The chemical symbol for neon is Ne. It is element 10 because it has 10 protons in its nucleus. Neon is called a noble or inert gas because it does not react with anything else. In nature, neon atoms never combine with other atoms to form new compounds.

Different colored neon lights can be made by adding other substances to the tubes.

Neon in Everyday Life

The most common use of neon is in lighting. In 1910, French scientist Georges Claude made red lights from glass tubes filled with neon, and realized the tubes could be bent into shapes to make the neon lights used for signs. The first neon sign was used over a Paris barber's shop in 1912. Neon gas is also used in lasers and as a **refrigerant**. Neon-filled tubes help protect transmission towers from lightning strikes.

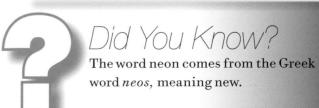

Did You Know?
The word neon comes from the Greek word *neos,* meaning new.

GLOSSARY WORD

refrigerant   a chemical used to cool refrigerators

Neptune

Neptune is the eighth planet from the sun. It is a gas giant made mostly of hydrogen and helium, and is a bluish color.

How Neptune Was Discovered

In 1613, Galileo Galilei first observed the planet now known as Neptune, but he thought it was a star. It was another 233 years before the planet was correctly identified. French astronomer Urbain Jean Joseph Le Verrier and British astronomer John Couch Adams independently worked out a likely location for a planet they believed must be located past Uranus. Le Verrier was the first to publish his calculated position of the unknown planet, in 1846. Shortly afterwards, German astronomers Johann Gottfried Galle and Heinrich Louis d'Arrest located Neptune within one degree of Le Verrier's predicted position.

Sun   Mercury   Venus   Earth   Mars   Jupiter   Saturn   Uranus   Neptune

Moons of Neptune Timeline

1846	1949	1989	2002–03
English astronomer William Lassell discovered Neptune's largest moon, Triton	Dutch-American astronomer Gerard Kuiper discovered another moon, Nereid	*Voyager 2* discovered six moons and confirmed the presence of rings	Five more moons discovered by a team of astronomers who combined images from telescopes in Chile and Hawaii

Naming Neptune

Debate raged over who should be credited with the planet's discovery, and what it should be called. Eventually, the traditional mythological name of Neptune, suggested by Le Verrier, was adopted. The ancient Roman god of the sea was thought a suitable name for a planet that looks blue. Neptune's moons are named after lesser sea gods.

Neptune Data

Average distance from sun	2,793,125,646 miles (4,495,100,000 km)
Diameter at equator	30,775 miles (49,528 km)
Composition	Thought to have core of rock and ice. Central mantle contains mainly water, ammonia, and methane. Atmosphere is mainly hydrogen and helium.
Moons	At least 13
Rings	Present
Mean temperature	−328 degrees Fahrenheit
Revolution around the sun	About 164 Earth years
Rotation on axis	16 hours 6 minutes
Gravity	About $1\frac{1}{10}$ times Earth's
Global magnetic filed	Present

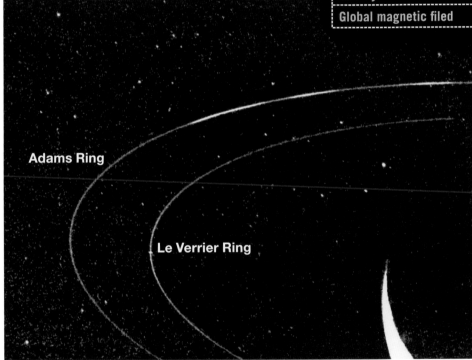

Adams Ring

Le Verrier Ring

Neptune's rings are named after people involved in its discovery: the Adams Ring is 39,146 miles (63,000 km) from the center, and the Le Verrier Ring is 32,932 miles (53,000 km) from the center.

Neptune's Winds

Neptune holds the record for the strongest recorded winds of any planet in the solar system. They reach speeds of up to 1,305 miles (2,100 km) per hour.

Urbain Jean Joseph Le Verrier (1811–1877)

Le Verrier was a French astronomer and mathematician who accurately established the exact orbits for the eight planets of the solar system. His valuable contribution to astronomy was recognized on France's 50 franc note.

Nitrogen

Nitrogen is a colorless, odorless gas. It makes up almost 80 percent of Earth's atmosphere.

How Nitrogen Was Discovered

In the 1770s, scientists knew that part of the air allowed things to burn, and part of it did not. In 1772, Scottish scientist Daniel Rutherford isolated a gas he called "phlogisticated" air from the part of air that did not allow things to burn. A few years later, French scientist Antoine Lavoisier recognized this gas as an **element** and called it azote, which means "without life." We now know this gas as nitrogen, and its chemical symbol is N.

In 1877, French scientist Louis Cailletet discovered how to turn nitrogen gas into liquid nitrogen: today, it is used to snap-freeze biological samples in laboratories, to freeze foods, and to freeze off warts.

Did You Know?

Nitrogen gas turns into liquid at –320.8 degrees Fahrenheit, and freezes into a solid at –346 degrees Fahrenheit.

Nitrogen and Plants

In the 1860s, French chemist Jean Boussingault discovered that adding nitrogen **fertilizers** to soil helped plants to grow better. He also discovered that plants called legumes can take nitrogen from the air and put it into the soil. Later, Dutch **microbiologist** Martinus Beijerinck discovered that bacteria living in legume roots changed nitrogen into a form that plants can use.

Legumes such as peas help to put nitrogen into the soil.

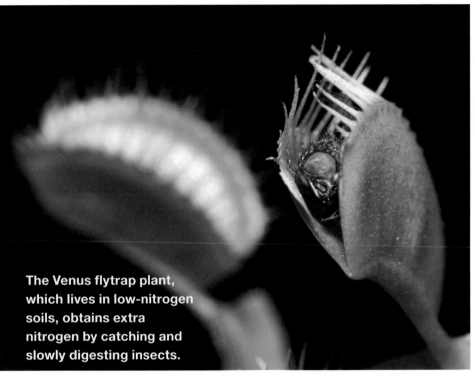

The Venus flytrap plant, which lives in low-nitrogen soils, obtains extra nitrogen by catching and slowly digesting insects.

Nitrogen in Everyday Life

Nitrogen is essential for the growth and survival of all living things. Plants get their nitrogen from the soil, and animals get their nitrogen by eating plants or other animals. Animals get rid of excess nitrogen in their urine, which is mainly water and urea. Urea is a **compound** containing nitrogen, carbon, hydrogen, and oxygen that can be used as a fertilizer.

GLOSSARY WORDS

element	substance made of only one type of atom
fertilizers	food for plants
microbiologist	scientist who studies bacteria and other micro-organisms
compound	a substance made of two or more elements chemically bonded together

Nuclear Energy

Nuclear energy is produced by splitting apart or joining the **nucleus** of atoms.

How Nuclear Energy Was Discovered

In 1932, English scientist John Cockcroft and Irish scientist Ernest Walton split atoms in two by bombarding them with **neutrons**. This process, known as nuclear **fission**, releases a large amount of energy. Cockcroft and Walton received the Nobel Prize for Physics in 1951 for this discovery.

Nuclear power plants convert nuclear energy into electrical energy.

Did You Know?

Australia does not have a nuclear power plant, but does have a nuclear research reactor. It is called OPAL and is operated by the Australian Nuclear Science and Technology Organization (ANSTO).

Chain Reactions

When scientists first split uranium atoms with neutrons, they discovered that two or three more neutrons were released from the uranium atoms. These hit other atoms, causing them to split and release even more neutrons, in a chain reaction that released a huge amount of energy in a very short time.

Nuclear chain reactions were used in atomic bombs during World War II. Afterwards, American researchers discovered how to slow down the chain reaction, so that the energy could be used for purposes such as generating electricity.

Nuclear fission occurs when the large uranium atom splits in two, releasing huge amounts of energy.

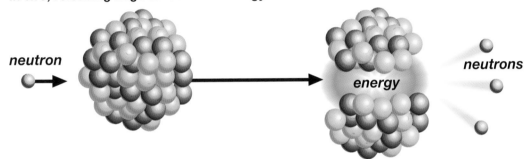

Nuclear Fusion

Nuclear **fusion** occurs when smaller atoms join together to form larger atoms, releasing energy. The sun is powered by nuclear fusion of hydrogen atoms to form helium atoms, releasing heat, light, and other forms of energy. Scientists have been researching controlled nuclear fusion as a way of generating electricity since the 1950s, but have not yet discovered how to do it.

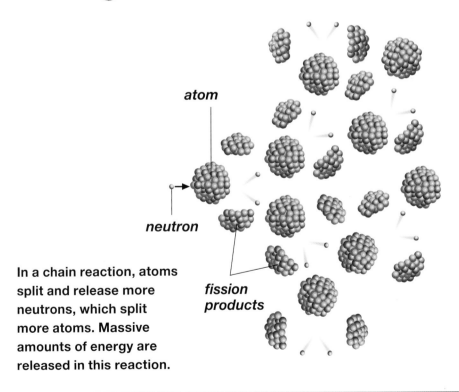

In a chain reaction, atoms split and release more neutrons, which split more atoms. Massive amounts of energy are released in this reaction.

GLOSSARY WORDS

nucleus	the center part of an atom that contains protons and neutrons
neutrons	particles found in the nucleus of atoms
fission	splitting into smaller parts
fusion	joining together

Oo Oil

Oil is also known as crude oil. It is an important energy source and the raw material for many everyday products.

Discovery and Uses of Crude Oil

Crude oil is a fossil fuel. It is the remains of microscopic once-living things that were changed by heat and pressure over millions of years. Ancient people discovered crude oil when it seeped to Earth's surface. The use of crude oil to bind rocks during wall construction dates back at least 4,000 years.

Crude oil can be collected from **reservoirs** under the ground by drilling wells and pumping out the oil. The first recorded crude oil discovery that required a well for oil recovery was in China, in 347. The oil was burnt to provide heat for evaporating **brackish** water to recover salt.

The world's largest oil producers are the Russian Federation, Saudi Arabia, and the United States.

Did You Know?

Crude oil is made up of hydrocarbon molecules, which are a combination of hydrogen and carbon atoms.

Modern Uses of Crude Oil

In 1855, American chemist Benjamin Silliman discovered how to obtain a range of products from crude oil, such as kerosene. Inventions such as the kerosene lamp, first made in 1857, then created a demand for these products. In the 1890s, the first commercial automobiles created a need for another byproduct – gasoline. Further uses of crude oil took the use of oil to 71.5 million barrels per day in 2007.

Our lifestyle is dependent on many crude oil byproducts such as gasoline, plastic items, paints, dyes, fertilizers, and even nylon fabric.

Crude Oil in Everyday Life

By 2007, only about 1.2 trillion barrels of proven crude oil reserves were left. Research into different energy sources is vital to maintain our way of life and to reduce greenhouse gas emissions from burning fossil fuels. We can also help by reducing our consumption of crude oil-based products.

GLOSSARY WORDS

reservoirs	large volumes of oil trapped under Earth's surface by rocks
brackish	salty

Oxygen

Oxygen is a colorless, odorless gas. It is the most abundant element in Earth's crust and makes up about 20 percent of the atmosphere.

How Oxygen Was Discovered

Oxygen was discovered by two scientists at almost exactly the same time. Around 1772, Swedish chemist Carl Scheele heated a variety of **minerals** and made a gas that allowed things to burn easily. He called the gas "fire air." About a year later, English scientist Joseph Priestly did the same. He noticed that as well as helping things to burn, the "fire air" allowed a mouse to stay alive longer than if it was in ordinary air. French chemist Antoine Lavoisier mistakenly thought that all acids contained the new gas. He called it oxygen, which comes from the Greek words *oxys* and *gene,* meaning "acid-producing."

Candles on a birthday cake burn oxygen when they are lit.

Did You Know?

Because oxygen atoms usually pair up to form molecules, the chemical symbol for oxygen is O_2.

Oxygen and Life

Oxygen is essential for almost all life on Earth. Plants take up carbon dioxide gas from the air through tiny holes in their leaves. At the same time, they release oxygen. After we breathe oxygen into our lungs, it enters our bloodstream and is carried by red blood cells to every part of our bodies. Without oxygen, we would die in three to four minutes.

Divers carry a supply of oxygen to breathe while under water.

Plants are vital for our survival, because they produce oxygen for us to breathe.

GLOSSARY WORD

minerals   rocks that contain metals combined with other substances

Ozone Layer

The **ozone** layer is a layer of Earth's atmosphere that contains high levels of ozone. It absorbs up to 99 per cent of the sun's damaging **ultraviolet radiation**.

Discovery of the Ozone Layer

French physicists Charles Fabry and Henri Buisson discovered the ozone layer in 1913. In the 1920s, British **meteorologist** Gordon Miller Bourne Dobson worked out how to measure ozone levels. He established a network of ozone monitoring stations around the world that are still used today. By 1930, British physicist Sidney Chapman had worked out how the ozone layer originated.

The Ozone Layer and Ultraviolet Radiation

An ozone molecule contains three oxygen atoms that are split apart by ultraviolet (UV) radiation and then rejoined in a continuous cycle. This process absorbs UV radiation, protecting much of the life on Earth. Most ozone is formed near the equator, but it is carried around the world by seasonal winds. The amount of ozone therefore varies around the world and at different times of the year.

Although the ozone layer absorbs nearly all of the sun's damaging UV radiation, we still have to protect ourselves against its damaging effects, which include sunburn and skin cancers.

Did You Know?

The ozone layer is found 9.3–15.6 miles (15–25 km) above Earth's surface. Scientists believe that the ozone layer has existed for 600 million years.

Ozone Depletion

In 1985, scientists discovered a hole in the ozone layer over the Antarctic. Polluting chemicals, especially chlorofluorocarbons (CFCs), were found to be responsible. By 1987, the Montreal Protocol international treaty was in place to phase out their production, and by 2003 scientists confirmed that the rate of ozone depletion had slowed.

1. UV light splits an oxygen molecule into two single atoms.

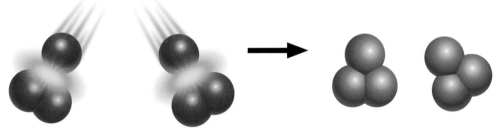

2. The single atoms combine with oxygen molecules to form ozone molecules.

The process of ozone creation (steps 1–2) and destruction (steps 3–4) absorbs up to 99 percent of UV light.

3. UV light splits an ozone molecule into a single oxygen atom and an oxygen molecule.

4. The single oxygen atom collides with an ozone molecule, forming two oxygen molecules.

GLOSSARY WORDS

ozone	a molecule made of three oxygen atoms
ultraviolet radiation	part of the sun's radiation that reaches Earth; also called UV light
meteorologist	scientist who studies the atmosphere and weather

Index

Page references in bold indicate that there is a full entry for that discovery.